Table of Contents

Introduction

These days there is a lot of talk about crypto art, nft and blockchain, also thanks to the stratospheric figures obtained by some digital artists at auction.

Crypto art is not new in its form: in fact, it mainly takes the form of 2D and 3D digital illustrations. The novelty lies in the formation of specific creative communities and, above all, in the market forms that support it. NFT is not a new artistic-expressive form, but a symbolic substitute aimed at creating a form of status without producing any material object. Beyond the form, the truly revolutionary act of crypto art thus lies in its ability to create a space of economic self-sustenance free from the art system. The debate, however, should not be about a trivially materialistic issue such as the real/digital duality, but rather about the nature that concepts such as reality and value assume today. Matter in the traditional sense is a tangible reality, but it is we who always delineate what is real, through more or less convincing symbolic productions and superstructures. Today we are all in some way producers and consumers of imagery; in this process we have our hands completely in the pie, and this continuous reconstruction and redefinition of reality becomes the key to reading the psychosis that is on the horizon. Crypto art is changing the face of something that lies on this line of flight, and the question could be not only artistic and ethical but also economic-political.

NFT
Investing

The Beginner's Guide to Investing in NFT (Non-Fungible Token). Create, Buy and Sell with Your Own Digital Crypto-Art and Collectibles.

© Copyright 2022 by **Jeff H. Bolton**

Jeff H. Bolton
NFT Investing

Legal & Disclaimer

The information contained in this book and its contents is not designed to replace or take the place of any form of professional advice; and is not meant to replace the need for professional advice or services, as may be required. The content and information in this book has been provided for educational and entertainment purposes only.

The content and information contained in this book has been compiled from sources deemed reliable, and it is accurate to the best of the Author's knowledge, information and belief. However, the Author cannot guarantee its accuracy and validity and cannot be held liable for any errors and/or omissions. Further, changes are periodically made to this book as and when needed. Where appropriate and/or necessary, you must consult a professional before using any of the suggested remedies, techniques, or information in this book.

Upon using the contents and information contained in this book, you agree to hold harmless the Author from and against any damages, costs, and expenses, including any legal fees potentially resulting from the application of any of the information provided by this book. This disclaimer applies to any loss, damages or injury caused by the use and application, whether directly or indirectly, of any advice or information presented, whether for breach of contract, tort, negligence, personal injury, criminal intent, or under any other cause of action.

You agree to accept all risks of using the information presented inside this book.

You agree that by continuing to read this book, where appropriate and/or necessary, you shall consult a professional before using any of the suggested remedies, techniques, or information in this book.

All information contained in this book is published in good faith and for general information purposes only. Any action taken by the reader on the information found in this book is strictly at his or her own risk.

Chapter 1: NFT What Are Non-Fungible Tokens

From the GIF of a cat that leaves a rainbow trail behind it to the first tweet in history, passing through a digital painting made up of 5,000 images, but also videos and music tracks: today on the Net everything that is created can be sold "in the form" of NFT.

In the beginning were kittens. The phenomenon of NFTs is not new and its genesis is firmly anchored to a very popular "craze": it was 2017 when the Canadian studio Dapper Labs developed CryptoKitties, a game based on the Ethereum blockchain that allows players to buy, breed and resell virtual kittens, each of which is unique (with its own genotype and phenotype), owned by users and endowed with a value that varies according to market trends (in 2018 a Kitty was sold for 140 thousand dollars). The game has caused an increase in transactions on Ethereum so much that it has come to cover 25% of the platform's traffic and generate a turnover equivalent to $19.6 million in a short time since its release.

What are Nft

The acronym for the term Non-Fungible Token means a set of digital information present within a blockchain that confers rights and characteristics to a specific entity. To simplify, it is a cryptographic token associated with a media that, once purchased, becomes a certificate of ownership and authenticity recorded in a blockchain.

To understand its meaning in more detail, we need to dwell on the meaning of the term "fungible" and its opposite: a fungible asset is a unit that is interchangeable with another of the same value.

The most striking example of this quality we can already do outside the categories of the blockchain.

Money, even money in the form of banknotes that we have in our wallets, is fungible by definition. If we were to give Joe 10 euros tomorrow and he were to give us another 10 euros, there would be no difference in the composition of our wealth. Each 10 euro bill represents an identical value. And for this reason money can be considered fungible.

On the contrary, an non-fungible element is endowed with its own specific economic-social individuality which does not allow its replacement with another. Therefore, a non-fungible token is in itself unique, not interchangeable and irreplaceable.

However, let's now think, for example, of a painting: it is a unique piece, there is nothing identical in the world. It can be sold for money, but it cannot be exchanged for an identical painting of the same value. A work of art is by definition non-fungible, because it cannot be exchanged for a generic good that is identical in value.

NFTs are the artwork, in our example, and classic cryptocurrencies such as Bitcoin are the money instead. If we exchange one Bitcoin against another Bitcoin, nothing will change in our asset compositions because a BTC is always identical to a BTC. In the case of owning an NFT token instead we will have a unique piece in our hands.

Any kind of media can be registered with an NFT, from music to videos, passing through texts, works of art, photos, even GIFs and memes. Once the NFT is purchased, the media continues to circulate freely on the network, but its rights become the property of the purchaser. The purchased token is therefore a certification of the media or digital work, not the work itself. NFTs therefore give a digital creation all the rights it would physically have as a work, such as rarity, authenticity, and ownership.

To use an analogy parallelism, an NFT would correspond to an autographed copy of an object, a sort of collector's item, but in a digital version.

On Blockchain

Just like classic crypto tokens, NFTs are also exchanged via blockchain. As you should be aware, the blockchain that currently supports them most frequently is Ethereum, which offers two different ERC standards for creating NFTs. As we will also get to see later, there are several projects and blockchains that allow you to create your own NFTs and exchange them.

The blockchain offers the advantages we all know for this type of exchanges: they are registered and searchable by everyone, they have solid mechanisms to validate transactions, and above all, they are freely accessible.

Which means that verifying the ownership of a given token is simple.

Metadata

An NFT includes meta-data, which accompanies the token with an image, file, audio track or any other type of data. The data is always freely searchable, at least on the most popular blockchains for this type of token. Nothing prohibits the incorporation of any type of data as a representation of title. It will go down in history, for example, the sale by Jack Dorsey, the founder of Twitter, of his first Tweet. Duly transformed into an NFT.

To represent the property

The most common use we can make of NFTs is to represent digital property. Most systems that support NFTs today allow you to tokenize a digital artwork, whether it's an image, or a song, or a video. Although the video is perfectly playable, as is the image or song, an NFT represents ownership of the same.

What are the benefits of NFT?

Among other advantages, these would be the main ones:

Standardization: digital assets were not represented until the advent of NFT. For example, collectibles were not represented in the same way as domain purchases. By having them represented in immutable "tokens," a set of standards such as ownership, transfer, and access control can be created.

Marketability: by standardizing NFTs, they can be easily traded. The new NFT design can be traded freely in the marketplace. Users can create more advanced trading features such as auctions, bidding, bundling, and the ability to sell in any currency. Not to mention the presence of traders generating a larger market.

Guaranteed Rarity: with smart contracts, NFT developers can create a limited number of any creation. They can also require that these special features remain constant over time. Unplayable tokens attest to the rarity of the original piece (which is highly valued in the art world).

Programmability: NFTs are 100% programmable. Many of them have complex mechanics because their design allows for many possibilities.

Chapter 2: How do NFTs Work?

Before we understand how NFTs work, let's take a step back, useful for those new to the industry, and talk about Blockchain.

What is Blockchain

With the term blockchain we identify a set of technologies that allow to maintain a distributed ledger of data (Distributed Ledger), structured as a chain of blocks containing transactions (and not only).

Each time a transaction is executed the consensus and change is distributed to all nodes in the network.

All nodes can participate in the process of validating transactions to be included in the ledger, so as to increase the authentication capabilities offered by the single blockchain.

A bit of history

The first blockchain-based transaction dates back to 2009, the year Bitcoin was born. The world's most famous currency was the first cryptocurrency to use a distributed ledger to keep track of all transactions, rewarding (again in Bitcoin) those who provided the computing power to generate new blocks to authenticate.

With the birth of Bitcoin, therefore, the blockchain as we know it today was also born: every transaction is legitimized by the decentralized network, without any control by authorities, banks or even just notaries.

The evolution of this technology is such that soon many services we were used to (notaries, banks, financial institutions) will go digital and can be managed in total security, using a distributed ledger to keep track of transactions and authentications.

How does Blockchain work?
Although services that leverage blockchain are increasing by the day, the underlying technology is similar across all platforms. This allows us to summarize how the technology works in 6 key points:

Decentralization: the information contained in the digital registry is distributed among multiple nodes, thus ensuring security and resilience of the systems even in case of attack on one of the nodes or in case of loss of a node.

Traceability: each item saved in the registry is traceable in every part and it is possible to trace the exact origin and any changes made over time, with absolute precision.

Disintermediation: the individual nodes of the blockchain certify the distributed information, thus making the presence of central bodies or companies to certify the data completely unnecessary.

Transparency: the content of the ledger is visible to all and can be easily accessed and verified by every node in the network but also through services that query the blockchain without making changes. No one can hide or modify data without the entire network learning about it.

Registry robustness: after adding a piece of information to the registry, it cannot be changed without the consent of the entire network.

Programmability: transaction operations can also be scheduled over time, so that certain conditions can be waited for before the entry or change is made.

All these conditions allow the technology to compete with the bodies and professionals that until now were in charge of certifying economic transactions (notaries and banks): the distributed ledger technology presents itself as a secure method of storing important information, computer inviolable, difficult to modify without leaving traces, and impossible to knock down as long as there are at least two blocks that can certify the information stored in the shared ledger.

What are Tokens?

By Token we identify a set of digital information that confers a property right to a party participating in a blockchain. We can define tokens as digital information recorded on a distributed ledger and representative of some form of right: ownership of an asset, access to a service, receipt of a payment, and so on.

The token can contain other rights and their set is governed by smart contracts.

Creating a token on the Blockchain means defining in a smart contract all its fundamental characteristics. Such as: the number of tokens in circulation, who is authorized to transfer them, those who can dispose of the tokens (the so-called "token holders"), the rules of access to the tokens.

Each token, ideally, can be built in a different way, although in reality some common standards have been adopted to simplify the creation of tokens (ERC20 and ERC721). Once tokens are created, they can be sent easily and without the need for anyone to keep track of different balances and transactions. Blockchain takes care of that, providing transparency and traceability: thanks to the technology's own features, anyone can see the code and verify that the tokens were created correctly. Moreover, some tools called wallets make it easy to manage and exchange them.

It is not difficult to confuse tokens on Blockchain with cryptocurrencies, the decentralized digital currencies that have made headlines thanks to the advent of Bitcoin,

Ethereum and numerous other projects. Here, too, it's good to put things in order.

In fact, there are tokens that are used just like currency. For example, their value can be pegged to that of traditional currencies. These tokens are called stablecoins and offer the same versatility and programmability as cryptocurrencies, but with the guarantees and stability of traditional currencies.

However, the purpose of tokens is not only to create digital currencies. We can divide the applications of tokens on Blockchain into two large families: fungible tokens on the one hand, related precisely to the idea of cryptocurrencies, and non-fungible tokens, on the other hand, related to objects and entities. (We will see later)

Smart Contract

The blockchain is also being used for smart contracts. These digital contracts are called "contractual type arrangements", an incorporation of contractual clauses managed not through words (as on the old contracts) but through computer language, thus incorporating computer protocols, algorithms or specific software.

These contracts are famous for starting automatically based on certain conditions decided by the parties at the time of signing: you don't even need to sign any piece of paper, since blockchains can certify the intentions of both parties involved.

This type of contracts are really futuristic, thinking about how much work is required to generate a traditional contract between two economic parties: the validity of smart contracts is provided by the blockchain technology itself, which elects itself as an impartial and incorruptible "judge" in guaranteeing the correct execution of the obligations and behaviors provided by the contract, as well as ensuring that the system where the contract is deposited is always active.

How a Smart Contract works

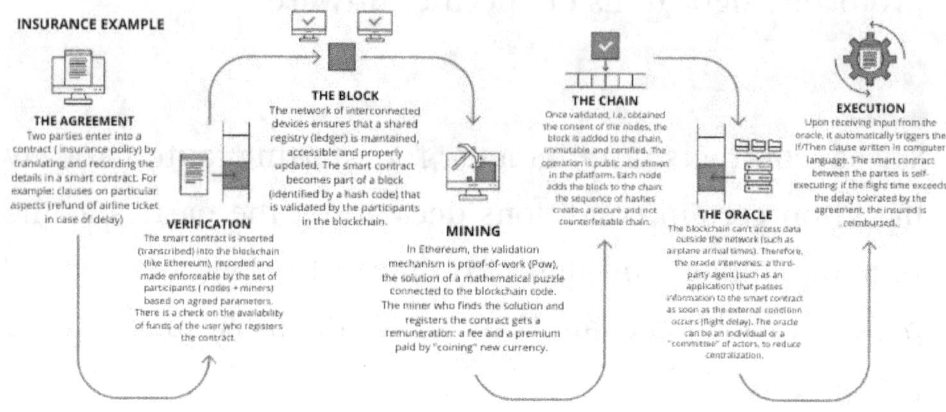

<u>Benefits and Limitations of Smart Contract</u>

It is in the structure of the digital ecosystem and in the decentralized architecture of the blockchain that we find the benefits and limitations of smart contracts.

The greatest benefit brought by the "Blockchain - Smart Contract" coupling is a considerable increase in efficiency; that is, the smart contract, when inserted within a blockchain, produces:

- Automation and legal certainty of the execution of contractual obligations visible to all participants of the network and not only to the parties involved;
- Transparency of the contractual obligations and of their results and implications such as to be pre-set and therefore "pre-comprehended" by all the participants of the blockchain;
- Immutability of the recorded transactions and therefore the impossibility to modify or cancel the contract;
- Possibility of finding an agreement in the absence of trust.

These features, in terms of efficiency, allow to:

- Save a considerable amount of resources in the negotiation and contract execution phases;
- Accelerate performance;
- significantly reduce the likelihood of disputes and disputes between the parties.

With respect to the latter aspect, it is evident that the formalization and execution of an exchange that takes place within the blockchain, due to the inherent characteristics of this technology, reduces the possibility of non-performance between the parties with the subsequent recourse to the court for legal protection. The structure and architecture of a system designed in this way helps to significantly increase the degree of certainty, security and stability compared to traditional contractual mechanisms.

The traditional contract finds its safeguard mechanism in its being legally binding, as it is protected by a normative source external to the contract, that is, by the legal system. In fact, it is the legal system that provides, in the event that one of the parties should be in default, the possibility for the losing party to take legal action to modify, cancel or enforce the agreed obligations.

The smart contract, unlike the traditional contract, places its binding mechanism in the peculiar technology of blockchain and smart contract that prevents from the beginning the default of the parties. It is technically impossible for the node to voluntarily violate the pre-established conditions.

However, among the most critical points of the smart contracts it is necessary to consider their irrevocability, which is triggered the moment they are inserted into the blockchain platform, from which follows the automatic execution of the performance that makes the exception of non-performance useless.

An expedient for the resolution of this issue could be given by a specific function, introduced by the most advanced blockchains (e.g. Ethereum), the so called kill or self-destruct function of the smart contract that aims to remove the programs no longer used, with the aim of improving the performance of the blockchain.

This function can be activated only by the node that created the smart contract, through the forwarding of a transaction and entering in the blockchain the corresponding electronically signed code, or, the parties could also insert the self-destruction function within the smart contract and in the event, provide, in a side agreement, the cases of activation of the same.

All of this allows the fulfilling party, in the event that the service is not provided, to take legal action to obtain contractual termination or even "deletion" of the contract from the blockchain through the self-destruct function.

The irreversibility of the transactions carried out by means of smart contracts would allow the parties to resort only to remedies of a restitutory nature, that is, fulfilling a performance to be carried out in specific form or for equivalent, where this is possible. The consequence is that, in the case of inalienable services, the party performing the service should be able to access the private key of the counterparty or the password of the computer where it is stored.

Two Types Of Non-Fungible Tokens

There are two distinct NFT standards. The first and most widely used, known as LRC721, is characterized by the trait of uniqueness. This means that a single contract is worth one token: a work sold through this standard is therefore a unique item.

The second standard, known as LRC1155, is characterized by the fact that one contract is worth multiple tokens. In this case, it is as if ownership is divided among several parties, as in the case of limited edition prints.

How NFTs Work

NFTs are based on the blockchain, a sharing technology that enables the storage and transmission of information or transactions by acting as a true "digital ledger", best known for Bitcoins but used in numerous other areas.

In terms of how NFTs work, the blockchain technology used is the same as that of Bitcoins. Unlike cryptocurrencies, however, NFTs cannot be traded directly with each other. This is because, as already explained, there are no two identical non-fungible tokens to which the same "value" corresponds.

Numerous are the attributes of NFTs. They are indivisible, i.e. they cannot be divided into smaller denominations and therefore exist only as a whole object. They are also indestructible: the data of non-fungible tokens, being stored on the blockchain via smart contracts, cannot be destroyed or removed. And they are verifiable: digital works of art, for example, can be traced back to their creator and thus authenticated without any need for third-party verification.

The buying and selling of NFTs can take place using different currencies, such as dollars or euros, since blockchains are fundamental to certify their authenticity but not for their exchange. In the last few months, numerous NFT marketplaces, real platforms for buying and selling non-fungible tokens, have appeared on the market, such as Nifty Gatewat, OpenSea, Known Origin, rarible.com and many others.

NFT token creation

The token is created on the Blockchain, incorporating a unique ID that represents it and with pointers to the metadata it incorporates. It is at this stage that we create a unique token, which is different from all other NFTs and is uniquely identified. The creation also assigns this token to a portfolio capable of doing ERC 721 token storage, or alternatively of the standard we have decided to use.

Bragging rights

NFTs definitely move the concept of ownership and possession into a whole new realm. If we were to look at the auctions that have been most successful in recent times, these are transfers of ownership of digital objects that are actually available to everyone. Everyone can still read the first Tweet in history, just as everyone can technically copy Beepsy's artwork that ended up at Christie's auction indefinitely.

What did those who bought these types of tokens actually acquire? Ownership in the strict sense, which since it does not offer in this case the exclusive enjoyment of the asset - which remains digital and accessible to all - has been considered by some commentators as a mere right to brag about the property itself.

In reality, there are many other levels involved in the use of NFTs. Think of cases like Decentraland, where NFT LAND tokens allow exclusive use and privileges over a virtual zone of the game. In that case one of the fundamental attributes of ownership, namely the power to be able to exclude someone, is fully preserved. The same can be said of systems, such as fan tokens, where possession of certain NFT tokens offers special privileges and access to merchandise. In that case, the NFT really gives the owner an exclusive right, which non-owners do not have.

To avoid the useless lucubration's we have already read in the non-specialized press, we invite everyone to focus, at least for now, on the strictly technological aspect of the matter. NFTs offer a safe, fast and cheap way to tokenize works of human ingenuity and to transfer them to others in a secure way. Whether we rely on the Ethereum or Tron network, or on the many niche systems, it doesn't matter.

It doesn't matter what will be the present and future fields of application of this technology. Because it is true that fashion has created auctions with closures almost impossible to understand for a reasonable mind. But it is equally true that these are in fact advertising operations in full swing, which have nothing to do with the actual future of this technology.

Chapter 3: What are NFTs for?

The initial reaction of anyone approaching the curious world of NFT for the first time is to wonder what is the point of acquiring - and consequently claiming - ownership of a file, since it can still be copied and "consumed" by everyone. We do not have univocal answers to the question, the fact remains that in the aleatory and intangible universe of the net, NFTs represent a way to assign value and authenticity (but also belonging) to the "objects" present in it. In doing so, the concept of exclusivity and rarity is introduced for the first time in the online world.

And exclusivity - although rather an end in itself - is what it is about, since with the purchase of an NFT you take possession of the file of a digital object and of the metadata that show that you own that object.

Certainly, with the creation of an NFT linked to a file destined to become popular, the possibility of "capturing" the value of viral content is opened wide.

The Risks

As you can imagine, even the glittering world of NFTs hides its thorny issues. There are many risks that can arise from their use, first and foremost the theft of digital artworks. As MalwareBytes reports, hackers recently breached the accounts of some users on the digital marketplace Nifty Gateway and stole artworks worth thousands of dollars, which were later resold on Discord or Twitter as NFTs. This is possible because the blockchain is designed to prevent counterfeiting, but not theft: if someone steals an NFT and resells it, the blockchain will record the sale irreversibly.

In other cases, some artists have reported that their works were stolen and resold on NFT buying and selling platforms without their knowledge or authorization, even realizing it long after it happened. The people who created the NFT probably "copied" the artwork from the artists' websites.

There is then another aspect not to be neglected, that is linked to the environmental impact of NFTs: not being able to disregard the blockchain, a notoriously energy-intensive system, even non-fungible tokens are automatically unsustainable.

Do NFTs Pollute?

The ecological theme seems to be one of the angles most used by detractors of the blockchain and cryptocurrency world to attack these types of systems. The same controversy has also been used to point out the ecological impact that systems like NFTs that are based on blockchain PoW would have. That is, the old way - exorbitant in terms of electricity and calculations - of validating new blocks of a blockchain.

The fact is that with the 2.0 upgrade, even the main blockchain that today supports NFTs will switch to a fully PoS system within a year, capable of consuming 1/100th of the energy while offering the same level of security. Even the green attack, which is actually already very poorly grounded today (one transaction of an NFT doesn't have this much impact), will have to surrender in the face of advancing NFT technology.

Trend or Revolution?

It is not yet clear what scenarios will emerge when the hype raised by NFTs dies down. What is certain is that the hype and the dizzying numbers accompanying their rise inevitably suggest a speculative bubble that could burst as easily as it was generated, as happened recently with the GameStop case.

It is also true that, especially in the world of digital art, many digital artists could find in NFT a new, concrete remunerative opportunity, seeing recognized the value of their work that would otherwise tend to get lost in the ether because of the extreme ease with which it can be copied and spread. A different matter for media such as GIFs, memes and social posts, whose commodification inevitably sounds bizarre and nonsensical to most people.

Whether a revolution or a passing fad, the NFT phenomenon attracts many and displeases just as many. We just have to wait and see what the future has in store for them.

A New Form Of Art

Among the first to take advantage of the technology were artists, who have found a relatively simple way to support their art, with fans who can finally fund works, which will remain, among other things, available to all. There are many artists, both digital and non-digital, who have relied on this type of technology to spread their works and find backers. Is the problem of the need for patrons solved even for less famous artists? Absolutely not, but the prospects offered by NFTs are certainly significant.

The case histories are countless and emblematic. Last March 11, a work by Mike Winkelmann, a digital artist known by the stage name of Beeple, was auctioned for $69 million at Christie's, making him the third highest priced living artist after Jeff Koons and David Hockney.

At the time the digital creation is acquired, the buyer receives the file with the work that incorporates a set of information including time of creation, size, print run and track record of any sales, including price and previous owners.

The work "Everyday - The First 5000 Days", a collage of five thousand digital "paintings" made by the artist, has raised a wind of revolution in the art market: not only is it the first NFT work to be sold by the historic auction house, but its sale also marks the official entry of a "digital object" into the traditional art circuit.

Chapter 4: How can NFTs enter everyday life?

NFTs, although very popular, are not yet part of everyday life for the general public. Or rather, they are slowly becoming so, also thanks to projects that already involve the world of sports, movies, video game collectibles. In addition, NFTs could also be used in the future for tracking supply chains and verifying the originality of clothing, something that actually already exists at a very popular sportswear brand.

Examples of some NFT uses

If it is true that NFTs are still something of a niche, it is equally true that there are already a lot of projects that make a concrete use of them. Here we will mention some of the most interesting projects that are already in full swing and that have demonstrated, if there was still a need, that in reality the world of NFT can offer a lot even to sectors other than speculation on art.

Decentraland and videogames

We have already spoken about it in the section specifically dedicated to the best NFT systems currently on the market. That of Decentraland can be a pilot case, that could be revised and improved by more commercially structured projects. It is not said that in the future we will not be able to see such systems applied to more popular games, such as World of Warcraft and all other MMORPGs of great success.

NBA Top Shot

The world of figurines and fantasy basketball has already moved, at least in part, to the NFT. The NFT Top Shots project is the proof. It runs on Flow infrastructure - of which we have already spoken within this guide - and distributes digital cards of the best NBA players against payment. And the strongest players, such as LeBron James, have ended up in the auction for six-figure values.

UFC: collectables

Even the wildly popular MMA circuit will soon make its debut on the Flow network, offering digital collectibles right through NFT technology. Another huge franchise that chooses the digital way of the future, recognizing how good a system of this type can offer to sports collectors.

Sorare: the global fantasy soccer

Another of the very interesting projects that today use NFT technology is Sorare, which offers a sort of fantasy soccer game on a global scale, which also relies on the world of NFT. Also in this case we are in front of a project definitely futuristic and that aims at the best possible technology for the management of multiple and even unique cards. We at Cryptocurrency.it have also talked about Cristiano Ronaldo's card that was sold for just over $290,000.

Nike and CryptoKicks

One of the most popular brands in the world of sports has long since started thinking about how to exploit the incredible NFT fad. And it has done it through the

CryptoKicks project, shoes tokenized within the Ethereum blockchain. The system in the future can also be used to certify the scarcity of certain collectible models and their originality.

Chapter 5: What does an NFT "contain"?

If we then go to examine more closely what the NFT "contains" we realize, however, that the data inserted are very few. Also for a question of energy used and space available, it is not possible to insert large files in the blockchain (which would end up weighing down the whole chain), but only a few elements (the hash of the file together with some properties).

So the owner of the Beeple work auctioned at Christie's (paid a whopping $69 million) now has a certificate hosted on the Ethereum blockchain that includes a unique identifier of the "contract" entered into. The certificate (not directly "written" in the blockchain but linked to it) will (likely) contain some properties of the token and the hash that links to a file that contains the image made by Beeple.

Some of these NFTs also contain the contractual conditions of the purchase, but more often these can only be found on the site that intermediates it (with the risk, however, that the complete discipline of the purchase ends up being lost when the platform's website goes down). Here the first problems begin.

Critical fronts

What will happen when hash functions are overtaken? As happened to the SHA1 function, which was fooled by Google itself, could it happen to the SHA256 function, which is the standard today? What will happen if the Ethereum blockchain were to be abandoned (and therefore no longer maintained by a collective of individuals who can effectively "outvote" anyone who tries to pass off as good a blockchain that is actually not genuine)? What will happen when the external content to which the links/hash contained in the smart contract point? Interesting technical solutions have been proposed to address some of the problems just outlined.

The technical solutions

For example, to avoid leaving the representation of the work sold to a hash/URL address, NFTs often make use of

IPFS (InterPlanetary File System) addresses. In fact, a simple URL may fail simply because the site operator stops paying for hosting or because they delete the file to make room for new content. And a hash may no longer be of any use when the file it refers to is lost.

IPFS addresses, on the other hand, are "links" to content on the IPFS network (a distributed file system, which we might associate in its operation with peer-to-peer file exchange systems). As long as someone on the IPFS network hosts that content, it can be found. This creates a potential multitude of hosts that ensures the file is maintained online, and this increases the likelihood that the content will survive over time. As for the different blockchains on which the NFT is hosted, it is clear that they will have to start providing some "guarantees" of survival if they want to gain market share.

If the Ethereum blockchain is likely to have an assured future also for the years to come, given that it moves a popular cryptocurrency and a smart contract system used for many different purposes, it is evident that the other competing blockchains will have to offer different types of assurances to "guarantee" their survival.

As the NFT phenomenon flourishes, moreover, investors will need to pay close attention to the blockchain on which the smart-contracts are hosted, to avoid buying certificates founded on improvised, poorly decentralized and consequently unreliable blockchains that may later be abandoned.

Chapter 6: Ways to make money with NFT

There are basically three ways to make money with NFT. These are three business models that, according to the NFT 2020 Annual Report, can provide a stable and sufficient source of income to make it a full-time business.

- Artist (digital content creator).
- NFT project development
- Trading NFT (investing in NFT)

Investing in NFT

Since they are perishable items, there is no organized market for investing in NFT. It is similar to investing in real estate or art.

There is no doubt that the art market can be a good source of income for those who know how to navigate it, but it lacks the transparency of an organized market.

Traders or investors in these projects follow the general rules of trading: buy low and sell high. But how can you determine if an NFT project has growth potential?

In this sense, the functioning of the NFT market can be compared to the art or cryptocurrency market: it is difficult to extract the value of assets. However, it can be considered that investing in NFTs is also even riskier than cryptocurrencies.

In fact, this market is too early to determine whether quick investments (short-term trading) are possible. However, if we look at the traditional art market, investments take time to mature. It is rare for a work of art to gain value in just a few years.

Although, looking at the evolution of the market, it is possible that the initial expectation creates excess demand and assets rise quickly, perhaps the waters will return to flow (the market always regains its sanity over the long term).

So, by treating NFTs as art investments, inflation can also play a role and influence investment returns. This would be a factor to keep in mind.

On the other hand, just as you analyze a company to determine its stock price, you can analyze the team of creators, the industry in which NFT moves, the community it generates, the creator's personal brand, and other key data.

You need to have a deep understanding of this market, just as you would with the real estate market or the art market.

Looking at the market capitalization of the various NFTs, you might think that the ones that are among the top are the ones that actually have a solid project.

Marketplace

If someone wanted to trade an NFT the choices are the most varied. The most accessible marketplace, based on Ethereum, is Open Sea, which claims to be the largest NFT marketplace. You can create and buy NFTs on the site, but you must have an Ethereum wallet to do so. The site offers to download a popular crypto wallet, MetaMask, which can be installed as a Chrome extension. Once set up you can buy the first ethers (in fact it is a currency exchange operation from euro to ether) to spend in non-fungible tokens.

If instead I want to "create" a NFT I can do it directly from Open Sea or from alternative sites like rarible, where the smart-contract that contains our work is sealed at a price that varies with the transaction costs on Ethereum.

An alternative that instead takes care of "selecting" the artists who can exhibit on its site is Nifty Gateway.

There are also many specialized marketplaces: if you want to buy an NFT of a historical moment in the history of the NBA, the site to consult is NBA Top Shot, while for the purchase of tweets the reference site is Valuables. For those who instead want to grab one of the cryptographic "kittens" that kicked off the NFT-mania still in 2017, the right site is CryptoKitties.

The Copyright Problem

A further critical point of the NFT market (which started with art but is moving to more and more disparate sectors, thus ending up forcing the legal mechanisms that regulate transactions related to works of art) is that of copyright.

First of all, in a global and unregulated market such as the NFT market, it is easy to imagine that cases of copyright infringement are on the agenda (especially when they are not the multi-million dollar transactions that make headlines), and that it is difficult to obtain protection, especially on a transnational level, with the difficulties of cross-border recovery of due compensation and conflicts between copyright laws further complicating the picture (especially if the transfer of rights is not clearly regulated and in any case is not included in the NFT).

It is also difficult in the digital art market not to talk about works derived from other works, of revisitations, of contaminations, which often create works of art that are a real nightmare when it comes to reconstructing the jumbles of copyrights that overlap.

In this sense, the example of the NFT that will be auctioned by Christie's and "created" by model and actress Emily Ratajkowski is significant. In deciding which work of art to include in a smart contract, Ratajkowski opted for a photograph that portrays her in front of a painting (created by a third party and of which the model owns a copy) which in turn reproduces a post on Ratajkowski's Instagram profile, which shows a photograph of the model taken for Sports Illustrated.

The provocation that this NFT represents is entirely legal and raises the question of whether Ratajkowski can legitimately transfer what is in fact a simple hash code of an image, even though she does not hold all the rights to the image itself (with regard to which Sports Illustrated, the photographer of the magazine, the painter who made a painting from the Instagram post, as well as the photographer who photographed the model thus creating the "collective work" that has become NFT could all claim rights).

For the future of NFTs, it is therefore essential to clarify what the purchased work is, and whether the object of the NFT is simply a hash code, or a link, or the digital work to which the previous references refer, or, finally, some or all of the rights to the work itself? From another point of view, it should also be considered that often, when selling an NFT, the author agrees with the buyer to obtain a percentage on each subsequent transfer of the good, a pact that is then "transferred" from buyer to buyer.

At an economic level, this is one of the most interesting strengths of this tech market, and is one of the not immediately perceivable traits that is determining its overwhelming success on the supply side. The impossibility of negotiating an NFT without going through a shared ledger (blockchain) guarantees maximum transparency for artists, who do not have to worry too much about the initial sale price of the work, being able to profit from the subsequent "changes of hand" of their creation and earn in proportion to any increase in the value of the asset.

Chapter 7: How to Create an NFT in 6 easy Steps

Step 1: Choose the work you want to tokenize

The first thing you need to do is choose the artwork. Non-Fungible Tokens can represent any digital file. You can make an NFT of a painting, text, music, video. Literally, anything that can be played as a media file. After all, the whole point of NFTs is to turn digital works of art into "one-of-a-kind" pieces in the age of infinite reproduction.

Step 2: Set up an Ethereum Wallet

There are numerous wallets to choose from to act as your public address and store your private key, but we generally recommend relying on a hardware wallet. (Trezor or Ledger).

Whatever the reason, you've decided you're going to get your fill while the crypto sun shines, you have the artistic skills to do it and the only thing you lack is the crypto know-how to get your work up there where the kind of people who will pay hundreds of thousands of dollars for a GIF can smile at your work and maybe shell out some money your way.

Well, you're in luck, because I've simplified the whole process into a few simple steps that will have your bizarre cryptographic art immortalized on the blockchain in no time.

If you're new to cryptocurrency, here's a quick crash course on how crypto wallets work: they're essentially software or hardware that helps you manage a public address on your cryptocurrency's blockchain. This public address is what stores your cryptocurrency and is viewable by everyone, although its ownership is completely anonymous (unless you do otherwise). Each public address has a private key that is used to deposit, withdraw, or send funds to and from the address. Think of it like a mailbox: everyone can see it, know where it is, and can send mail for it. But only the person with the key to the mailbox can open it and retrieve the contents.

There are two types of wallets: Hot Wallets that are connected to the Internet and provide more convenience to the user at the expense of less security and Cold Wallets that store your information offline and are less convenient for frequent use but provide much more security for the user. A popular example of a hot wallet is commonly used MyEtherWallet, while the best examples of cold wallets are hardware-based wallets from Trezor or Ledger. Yes, good old pen and paper can also work as a cold wallet, although you'll have to generate your own public addresses which can be a problem.

We recommend MyEtherWallet or MetaMask for users who are new to cryptocurrencies and just looking to put their work up for sale, or any of the Trezor / Ledger hardware wallets for those interested in cryptocurrency storying in general (as well as those who have created a significant value sale and would like to keep their earnings safe!).

Note that Foundation only connects to MetaMask.

Step 3: Buy some Ether

Once you've chosen your file, you need to buy some Ether.

You can do NFT on different blockchains, but for simplicity's sake we'll talk about Ethereum here. It's the most popular network and the most important NFT marketplaces support it.

Minting an NFT might cost you some money. Therefore you need an Ethereum wallet on which you will have deposited at least some Ether (the cryptocurrency based on Ethereum). One of the easiest to use is called "MetaMask". You can download it as a free app on your iPhone or Android smartphone. The price charged to create NFT is highly volatile. It's good to have at least $100 worth of Ether on hand, with the understanding that the minting process could cost even more depending on the daily operating price.

On OpenSea, one of the largest marketplaces, the process is free because of the type of tokens the platform creates at the time of "minting." You still have to connect a wallet to create an account.

Step 4: Choose a marketplace

Now that you have everything in place, you need to choose a marketplace where you can physically (virtually?) create your NFT and then offer it for sale.

The most popular ones are Mintable, Rarible or OpenSea. For the sake of this guide, we'll choose the last one because it's free and has no moderation on the content you can put up for sale. This means that you don't have to be approved as an artist to sell on the platform. It also means that the marketplace is full of digital junk that no one will ever buy.

On OpenSea, click on the user icon, then click on "My Profile." On this page, you can choose how to link your ETH wallet to proceed. If you're using MetaMask, you can connect it to the platform by selecting "Use a different Wallet" and then clicking on WalletConnect. The process is relatively simple. Follow the platform's directions, then confirm the Wallet Connect transaction by "signing in" from your MetaMask app.

Step 5: Upload your Art

Once you've connected your ETH portfolio to OpenSea, you can proceed to create your first NFT. Click on "Create" in the top menu, and create a collection. Fill in all the necessary information, then save. You are now ready to begin the actual process of minting a new NFT. Click on

New Item, upload your artwork, and provide all the details you need. Once you're ready to proceed, click Create.

Congratulations, you have successfully created a non-fungible token! To sell it on OpenSea, though, you'll need to open the item you just created in your collection and click the sell button. On the page that follows, you'll be able to choose the Ethereum tokens you'll accept as payment, decide whether you want to sell at a fixed price or auction, and the percentage of royalties you want to receive from the first and subsequent sales.

Step 6: Pay the Transaction Fee

With your NFT graphic locked and loaded, all you have to do is pull the trigger on the gas and you can sit back while your work is uploaded to the blockchain and becomes a unique entity on the network, immutable and invulnerable to any server collapse. The transaction fee will ensure that your NFT is mined by whatever Ethereum miner withdraws the contract, pocketing your commission for their troubles.

After that, it should only be a matter of a couple of minutes before your newly minted NFT is available and on the market just waiting to make the day for the sharp patron who sees it first!

Profit (?)

Okay, so you've managed to create an NFT, and successfully placed it on the OpenSea marketplace. Now what? Waiting for someone to notice your precious token won't get you very far. You'll need to market yourself and make the item appealing to buyers, possibly to an existing community of people interested in your work. This is the most challenging part, and it has nothing to do with the artistic process itself. Yes, it's just as ruthless and selective as the physical art world. Unless you're a character in a meme or some other internet phenomenon. In that case, congratulations: you've probably found a way to make money off that embarrassing photo that people have always used to make fun of you.

Main Marketplace

OpenSea. It is a platform to sell and buy Nft founded in 2017. It is used by logging in with a wallet like MetaMask. Everyone can sell and buy Nfts without special permissions, mostly using the cryptocurrency Ethereum (Eth) for payments or adding their own tokens. Nfts can be sold on an auction basis and each bid must be at least 5% higher than the previous one. The auction can be open, have an auction base or be closed by the seller when he is satisfied with the bet obtained. On OpenSea it's possible to put on sale both single Nft, or in one copy, or more copies of the same work or even entire series.

SuperRare. You have to pass an interview to start selling your works on this platform. The SuperRare team makes sure that the works are original, created by real artists and, as the name says, that the Nfts are very rare and therefore created only in one copy. Here, in fact, you can only sell single works and not entire series. Who buys has free access to the platform, needing only to connect with MetaMask to be able to buy and participate in auctions. The standard are payments in Ethereum. For artists, the platform retains 15% of sales on the primary market and 10% on the secondary. For collectors, for each bid (offer) will be paid the fee (tax) to the Ethereum blockchain, which these days also reaches $ 40-50. This fee, of course, is lost and spent even if you don't win the auction. Includes Nft of art and non-art.

Nifty Gateway. Compared to other platforms here purchases can also be made using normal credit card. MetaMask is supported, but to make onboarding easier, Nifty Gateway has decided to enable payments in fiat currency as well. Instead, for those who sell their works, monetization will be done in USDC stablecoins. Sotheby's partner in digital auctions.

Makersplace. Selling, collecting and investing: MakersPlace is the platform for digital artists and collectors who want to be part of the new frontier of the market. Founded by Dannie Chu, Yash Nelapati and Ryoma Ito, Makersplace's marketplace is growing rapidly, increasing sales and members by 30% per month. Accepts credit cards.

Rarible. The first Nft art marketplace to implement a token that incentivizes trading. It's called Rare and allows the most active creators and collectors on Rarible to vote for any updates to the platform and participate in its management. It includes Nft of art and non-art.

Decentraland. It aims to create a virtual world where users can have complete control over the content they create and share, giving them all the tools to independently monetize their work. It is a three-dimensional world navigable by users using the browser or with the aid of virtual reality visors. The world is divided into 90 thousand lands that represent the digital spaces that users can buy, sell or rent to share content. All interactions in the platform are mediated through a token called Mana, whose value, in recent weeks, has grown over 180%.

König Gallery. The famous physical gallery König Gallery has also recreated its gallery (the very structure of St. Agnes in Berlin) on Decentraland by hosting a group exhibition with paintings and digital sculptures in the form of Nft. It is the first physical gallery to open a location on the famous Ethereum blockchain-based platform.

Palm. Ethereum and ConsenSys co-founder Joe Lubin announced the launch of Palm, an alternative network for Nft that is 99% more energy efficient. Among the blue chip artists the first to take part in the project is Damien Hirst with "The Currency Project", a series of 10 thousand oil paintings on paper created five years ago and transformed into Nft. At the moment the starting figure for the sale is not yet known.

Chapter 8: Small Handbook for Becoming a Crypto Artist

A crypto artist is an artist who creates digital artworks, exhibits them in digital galleries and eventually sells them in exchange for digital currency (cryptocurrency). Here's my (very personal) little handbook for becoming one:

1. create a physical work of art and digitize it or give life to a digital native work. A language designed for generative art is Processing. A JavaScript library for doing the same things on the web is p5.js;

2. every work of art has a (good) story to tell (otherwise you wouldn't have made it). Write it on Medium;

3. open a digital cryptocurrency wallet. This is the trickiest part because it has to do with money (digital and real). I recommend MetaMask from desktop or cipher from mobile. You'll have a public key (a kind of IBAN, if you compare it with current account) and a private key (a kind of PIN

to access your account). Never reveal your private key, just mark it on a piece of paper and put it in a safe place (which you will be able to find!). No one but you knows your private key, so if you lose it you have lost your wallet. You can instead give your public key to receive payments or other digital works;

4.   display your work in a digital gallery. KnownOrigin and SuperRare are currently my favourites. To enter these galleries, it is necessary (but not sufficient) to have a digital wallet. Exhibiting your work is not immediate, each gallery carefully selects the artists they exhibit. Make yourself known first by frequenting their social networks;

5.   if you have been published, i.e. your work is exhibited, cross-link your work in the gallery to your story on Medium. I'd be curious to read the story behind the work, or see the work behind the story;

6.   periodically check to see if there are any offers to buy your work; if you are happy with the offer, sell the work (remember that offers can be withdrawn). You will find that it is a bit painful to

deprive yourself of a work that you have created with such passion and that you feel is yours, even if it is digital and therefore ephemeral. This supports the hypothesis (which I support) that digital art is an authentic art form. Remember that you can also donate your artwork (and receive artwork as gifts). Be generous;

7. don't disinvest the digital currency, but use it, for example to create a small collection of digital artwork or to make donations. This way you will feed the digital art market and give back to artists.

The 3 Best Online Software For Artists

There are some online software that can greatly simplify the work of artists, from the management of works to social content. Let's find out which ones!

On the web every day, software, applications and start-ups are born that aim to simplify one or more activities, even related to the art world.

For an artist, however, it can be easy to get lost in this magnum sea, and you risk wasting a lot of time figuring out which tools can be truly functional.

However, there are some great software, easy to use and affordable, that help artists in their daily activities.

Let's see which are the 3 best ones:

Canva: this tool allows you to produce graphics, content and short videos/animations for social media but also for marketing material. It's very easy to use thanks to a drag & drop system, starting from a series of present templates.

For the artist, not skilled in more complex tools like Photoshop or Indesign, this app is very useful to create posters for exhibitions and events, or content for social media, or even to easily customize your resume or portfolio. Canva also allows you to share your project with a team of users, for example in the case of an exhibition or an exhibition event, with the gallery owner and his staff;

Ilovepdf: very useful software for merging pdf files into a single document, but also for converting jpg or excel into pdf and vice versa. For an artist, this tool can be useful for the creation of documents such as curriculum and portfolio, but also business plans for exhibitions or events;

Art Rights: is the first platform for the management and certification of works of art to support artists, collectors and professionals. Thanks to Blockchain technology and Artificial Intelligence, the software allows artists to enter information about their artworks by creating an Art Rights Certificate, which becomes the "passport of the artworks". The artist will be able to share this information with other gallerists, collectors, and other professionals, who can confirm it, increasing the value of the artwork and allowing it to be tracked throughout its history. Art Rights is also a management software, which allows you to catalogue and digitize an unlimited number of works of art, creating a true digital archive.

Then there are other softwares such as Trello, which supports the organization of daily activities, and Hootsuite useful for scheduling and managing social media content.

Being a professional artist also means being attentive to technological innovations, as apps and platforms can significantly reduce the time spent on certain activities, allowing you to devote more resources to real artistic research.

Chapter 9: NFT Market, 5 Projects with Potential

If bitcoins introduced the concept of cryptocurrency and trust less (digital rarity), NFTs, also referred to as crypto collectibles, highlight the concept of digital rarity even more, being unique and limited in quantity. This has helped developers solve the problem of ownership of digital objects.

NFTs are applicable to numerous projects and, according to statistical studies, are distributed:

- 41% - gaming industry
- 29% - collectibles
- 13% - real estate
- 7% - collectible card games
- 6% - domain names
- 4% - art

Among the first successful NFT projects is CryptoKitties, which in 2017 congested Ethereum's blockchain, allowing players to collect and trade virtual cats. The project is the first fun example of blockchain use involving gamification and not currency: a guaranteed success that has created a multi-million dollar market.

Not only gaming, the artwork sector also encountered a boom in 2021.

The main NFT branches include gamified collectibles with playback functionality (such as CryptoKitties), pure collectibles, images and collectibles based on sports and art. Images accompanying Ethereum-based NFTs include algorithmic variations and their price depends on rarity and special features.

Latest NFT Market Trends

Cryptopunks

The existing 10,000 CryptoPunks represent a simplified art form that has depopulated the market, becoming one of the top collections, even following promotion on social media. A great choice for those looking to invest in NFTs thanks to the thriving resale market, due to the mix of scarcity and growing popularity.

Just think that recently one of the very rare alien characters traded at 605 ETH or $761,889.

Pascal Boyart

Pascal Boyart is an established artist, famous for his murals on the streets of Paris. The OpenSea storefront, the largest digital marketplace for NFTs and crypto-collectibles, has sold some of the artist's works for a value of over 400 ETH and, the new images are minted in NFTs and sold at auction. In just a few months, the artist has managed to create a crypto-space for himself, making an art marketplace to gather customers interested in his pieces.

Lil Moon Rockets

Lil Moon Rockets is an emerging NFT project that combines vector art with algorithmic genealogy. A blind sale model is used whereby all artwork will be revealed upon contract conclusion.

Unlike other NFT projects built around the Ethereum blockchain, Lil Moon Rockets uses Binance Chain, which offers easier purchases with lower fees, to issue its NFTs and "name your rocket" tokens.

Beeple

Beeple is a digital artist who has achieved outstanding performances in the NFT market. One of the biggest successes was an animation with a mutation feature inherent in the outcome of the 2020 US presidential election, which sold for $6.6 million.

Hashmasks

Hashmasks is one of the most well-known projects in the NFT scene. The collectibles combine alien or robotic figures with backgrounds, presenting a post-modern aesthetic. More than 16,000 images have been combined through the work of artists and the algorithm.

These masks are now becoming a sign of identity in social media games. The most expensive mask has reached the price of 420 ETH and users can make them even more unique by renaming them.

Digital collectibles offer new possibilities for blockchain technology and the NFT market could become crucial for the development of the blockchain ecosystem and beyond.

Chapter 10: How to Evaluate an NFT Collection

In this chapter, we will discuss what elements to analyze to assess whether a collection has potential and whether its value can grow over time after the public sale.

Let's start with how to evaluate the NFT collection to see if it is worth participating in the public sale. These evaluations are purely subjective and should not be considered as absolute rules for investing in the NFT world. On the contrary, being a highly speculative world, it is very risky to operate and there are good chances to lose all the money you decide to invest.

On the other hand, if you are a digital artist, you can, maybe earn some money, using NFTs to sell your digital artistic creations.

Communication Channels

The two most used communication channels in this market are Twitter and Discord. This allows you to follow new projects closely.

Twitter.

Projects use this channel to share the most important news, make announcements, and interact with users who decide to follow the project.

You can think of Twitter as a news outlet, a specific Ansa that makes short announcements about its development for each individual project. For example, there are announcements, contests, collaborations, dates and times for pre-releases and public sales, etc.

Discord.

This is a virtual place to interact with other users interested in the project and supporters of the project.

Usually each project will create its own server on Discord, where different channels are divided. Channels can be open to everyone, restricted to specific users only or locked, which means only administrators can write in them.

Discord is the beating heart of the project.

While on Twitter you can find out about new announcements and news, on Discord you can delve into information and participate in the "life" of the project.

When you're investing $1/200, if not $4/5000 for a virtual video or image, it's probably time to dig deeper.

Discord is the perfect place to find information and communicate with other users. Furthermore, Discord is also a channel where you can grow your community and one of the things that actually contributes to the success of your project is the community you create around your project.

In conclusion, regular users who decide to invest, or intend to invest in a particular NFT collection, follow Twitter to get quick updates on the development of the project and go to the Discord server in order to learn more about it.

So, if you want to keep your finger on the pulse of the situation, you need to know how to act on Twitter and Discord. Obviously, without an account for these channels, access will be denied.

From whom is the NFT collection suggested?

To understand the potential of a project, you need to know who is talking about or advertising a particular NFT collection. That is, to understand if the information has come from a reliable and authoritative source.

In fact, if I read the news that a famous person we'll call X bought a Crypto Y nft for 70 thousand dollars, I'm pretty late if I want to invest too and I don't have big capital. When a collection or an NFT reaches a certain popularity, its value has already grown exponentially, so there is little left for small investors (although it is not to be excluded that it may grow in the future).

On the other hand, if an "influencer" on Twitter, daily suggests a new NFT collection, it is possible that there is a possibility of investment but above all of gain and I'm going to analyze the project in more detail.

In fact, very often influencers tend to emphasize the potential of a project, especially by virtue of the fact that that project has paid them to make people talk about their NFT.

Then there is an infinity of sites that talk about NFTs that can suggest interesting projects. For example on Rarity.tools or on Cryptofoxtrot they show, in advance, nft collections about to start with the public sale.

In these cases it is necessary to do more in-depth research and draw the right evaluations.

How to Evaluate the Project

Evaluating the project is not easy, in fact there are projects with ad hoc mounted and others natural.

To understand whether a project's construction is mounted or natural, three things must be evaluated:

1. Twitter channel
2. Discord server
3. Website

Twitter

Follow the project's Twitter channel about the new NFT collection, so you can stay updated on developments.

Therefore, if the Twitter channel of a 10 thousand NFT collection has a few hundred followers or a few thousand (like 2 or 3 thousand), it lets us know if the project may have a large following or not.

Conversely, if there are Twitter channels with an impressive number of followers, but few tweet interactions. For example, if a Twitter profile with 20 thousand followers, but few likes per tweet, then, there is something wrong.

You can use this tool to evaluate a portion of a Twitter profile's followers: https://www.followeraudit.com/fake-follower-audit.

In some circumstances, Twitter numbers are inflated for two reasons:

- followers have been bought
- the followers have been abused incentives to follow the profile (ex: follow the Twitter profile to receive a free NFT and tag 5 friends)

Finally, I'm looking to see if the numbers diverge much from the server numbers on Discord.

Discord

Discord is even more important than Twitter, because here you can interact with other users and read more in-depth announcements and news released by the developers of the project.

Even on Discord you can inflate the numbers, but you can easily understand. In fact, just see how active users are in the various channels within the server or compare the numbers with Twitter.

A Discord server with 80 thousand members and a Twitter profile with a few thousand, is hardly credible.

Website

The website is the element that least helps to understand the validity of a project. In fact, it is possible to find very poor sites, but have been able to build a good community, for example the NFT project Lucky Sloths has a horrible site, but has been able to grow the value of its NFT from a minting price of 0.01 ETH to over 0.08 ETH.

Other projects have appealing sites, for example Vault of Gems, but have not been able to sell-out the collection, getting stuck in a kind of limbo.

Tips for Purchasing NFT

1.   If the project is good, the numbers between Twitter and Discord will be similar and the interactions will be appropriate for the number of followers. If these numbers are not balanced, we are probably facing a hype, so you have to discard the project. In a nutshell, there are no shortcuts, to grow the community you have to do a lot of advertising and not buy followers.

2.   The second aspect to consider when evaluating the purchase of an NFT is its minting price. Let's take as an example the Bored Ape Yacht Club collection (whose current minimum market price is about 28 ETH), the minting price for a single NFT during the public sale, which took place at the end of April 2021, was 0.08 ETH. Subsequently, for about a month the price remained below 1 ETH and then increased exponentially in August. Other projects, however, decide on a much higher minting price. In fact, the NFTs in the Logan Paul Digital Collectibles Store collection had a minting price of 1 ETH at the time of the public sale. Since then, the price for the NFTs in this collection has continued to drop, never returning to the initial value. Why the difference between the two

collections? On one side there is Yuga Labs, a virtually unknown company and on the other side there is a world famous youtuber. Logan Paul, thanks to his fame, has set an exaggerated minting price. Quickly cashing in on the proceeds of the collection without then caring about the future of the collection. In fact after the launch of the collection the publicity for the project disappeared and potential buyers were no longer willing to purchase an NFT from the collection at 1 ETH. Instead, the launch of the Bored Ape Yacht Clubs had much less publicity and the minting price was significantly lower. This is because otherwise, by the law of demand, no one would have been willing to buy NFTs since they were made by an unknown company. The Yuga Labs team then worked to increase interest in the collection to increase the desire to own NFTs, thus increasing the market price. Essentially, while the supply of NFTs has remained the same, the demand has increased, so potential buyers are willing to offer higher prices to purchase NFTs from the collection. Meanwhile, Yuga Labs makes money from secondary market royalties; in fact, the team earns a percentage of each NFT collection sold.

3.   Coining price rule. In order to evaluate the initial mintage price of a single NFT, one must consider if the launch hype is highly emphasized and the mintage price is high (when it exceeds 0.1 ETH) it is difficult for the price to rise further in the secondary market. Therefore, the rule is to find projects that have a good emphasis and whose initial minting price is in the range between 0.01 and 0.1 ETH.

4.   Number of NFTs to be minted. Another one to consider carefully is the number of NFTs a single wallet can mint at the time of public sale and the maximum number of transactions it can perform. Suppose a set consists of 10,000 NFTs, each with a minting price of 0.08 ETH. In this hypothetical case, the cost to mint the entire collection is 800 ETH or about $2.5 million. For a wealthy collector, minting most of the collection is not a problem if there are no restrictions. Without limits, we would be faced with an oligopoly of a few collectors trying to sell at sky-high prices, or this would lead to the death of collecting itself, since most of the value had already been given by the community that had formed around it.

5.   Maximum number of NFTs. Better to buy collections where each individual wallet cannot mint more than 10 NFTs. This is to avoid that there are few users who can grab most of the works.

It is better to buy NFTs from a collection that allows a larger number of users to enter, as this will increase the value after the public sale.

In conclusion

The world of NFTs is a wild new world you have to be very careful not to buy a file that is not worth anything.

Here, in summary, are the rules for evaluating whether a specific NFT in a collection is worth buying:

- Who suggests the collection?
    - ~ an influencer against payment
    - ~ a site that lists future public sales
- Has a launch strategy been built around the collection?
    - ~ Is it a hype, or is it real
    - ~ Is there a community enthusiastic about this project?

- Will there be potential buyers who are willing to spend more in the future to buy one of these NFTs?
- How many NFTs can a wallet mint? Is it possible to prevent a few users from buying most of the collection?

By analyzing these points and answering these questions as objectively as possible, you will be able to figure out if it is worth participating in a public sale.

Chapter 11: NFT and Real Estate

Virtual Real Estate

The endless possibilities that NFT technology offers were recently exploited to create the first "Non Fungible Token" home in the history of the virtual real estate market.

"Mars House," is the name of contemporary artist Krista Kim's "built" virtual property, a property that sold for $500,000.

"Mars House" is designed with sharp lines and rounded edges, furnished with glass furniture and surrounded by a digital Martian landscape, from which it takes its name.

The new owner of "Mars House" will receive the unique file of the design and be able to upload it into multiple 3D immersive worlds to experience the digital space through virtual and augmented reality. Kim's vision is for the NFT real estate market to become parallel to the real one so much so that his digital art will also be accessible to those who prefer to touch their purchases. The home's furniture, in fact, can be built in replica in real life by selected Italian glass furniture manufacturers.

Comparison of traditional and digital area investment

To better understand the opportunities of investing in digital land assets through NFT, we will compare digital land to traditional land investing.

A key feature of blockchain innovation is that it eliminates middlemen and the additional time and cost they entail.

Digital land NFTs can be managed by smart contracts; a program that runs on the blockchain, can receive and send transactions and is immutable. A smart contract automatically executes and completes tasks within the pre-determined terms of the contract.

Smart contracts offer ease of use. You can enter into an agreement without trust and automatically release the NFT from the seller to the buyer after the funds have been deposited.

In comparison, traditional land requires a significant investment of time and effort, and contracts are typically signed by multiple intermediaries. With physical resources, specialists are usually needed to determine the value, worth and condition of the asset.

Digital assets can be bought and sold quickly: no visits are required to investigate the quality and site of a physical asset, and the cost of acquisition is reduced to a small fraction of a traditional land investment.

The originality of the digital asset is encoded in the NFT, and buyer/seller interactions are handled automatically by a blockchain-based smart contract. Time-consuming title searches and property history checks are replaced with rapid transactions.

Trading assets through smart contract-based NFTs offers so many benefits that it is likely that the industry will evolve in the future to allow the purchase of physical land and real estate.

This would reduce costs and simplify the issuance of title insurance for banks and all parties involved in the transaction. But for now, digital land investments are uniquely positioned to benefit from the key advantages of investing and transacting on the blockchain.

Cash

Liquidity measures how easy it is to convert an asset into cash.

Land and real estate are often large, illiquid investments. They require a significant amount of funds to purchase and are relatively illiquid.

You can't cash out your investment where and when you want. There are many restrictions, permits and challenges you may face as you develop or sell the land and it may take years to sell land or property.

Because they are digital assets, NFTs are much easier to trade and convert to cash than traditional land and real estate assets.

They can also be minted - created - on one platform and then traded on multiple markets. This creates more opportunities for potential buyers from all international markets than is feasible with traditional assets.

And as the NFT investment market matures and develops, opportunities to borrow against your digital terrestrial asset are likely to emerge. Digital asset securities are in the early stages, but options already exist to use them as collateral.

While initially only cryptocurrencies like Ethereum could serve as collateral for a loan, digital assets including NFTs for art, collectibles, and domain names are now being included as collateral-worthy assets.

The inclusion of digital assets as collateral means that as the NFT and DeFi[1] sectors continue to evolve and mature, the liquidity of digital assets will expand over time.

No maintenance cost

Maintaining and maintaining traditional land and property can be expensive; you will be required to pay property taxes and other expenses.

You may have to pay to maintain the land or property, such as regularly mowing the lawn or cleaning and repairing the property. If left undeveloped, the quality of the site will deteriorate, wildlife will take over, and environmental problems such as flooding or leaks may occur.

---

[1] DeFi (Decentralized Finance) Decentralized finance - is the organization of services, similar to banking, on infrastructures that assume the absence of hierarchies, such as blockchain or that are otherwise less centralized than the banking system.

In addition, land alone does not generate income. Developing the land to a point where it generates income could be expensive and risky as an investment. For these reasons, it can be very challenging to get a loan on vacant land; there's a good chance you'll have to pay up front, committing significant funds to the investment.

Digital assets, on the other hand, do not require maintenance and upkeep costs. You can choose to hold on to your asset as its value increases over time as the digital platform grows, or sell or develop your digital asset to generate revenue without additional costs and fees.

Phergyson, an avid digital land trader who proudly calls herself a "faux real estate magnet," says owning digital land is "definitely" easier than owning real estate. There are "no closing costs or recurring costs for taxes and repairs. And, most importantly, no plumbing."

Traditional land use

The government can restrict the use of a land asset, with rules for the type of property or ways the land can be developed.

If you're buying land for residential or commercial development, you'll first need to make sure the land has all the necessary permits and check the conversion regulations.

There may be instances where land use restrictions may limit the ways in which the owner can use the land. Whether it is for horticulture, recreational purposes, or real estate development, obtaining permits and documents is often a lengthy process.

The availability of utilities could also impact development opportunities. How easy is it to set up a sewer system, running water, electricity, gas, phone, cable and internet?

Depending on the location of your land, access to necessary utilities could be expensive and limit potential development.

Digital Land Use

Digital land, however, offers multiple opportunities to monetize the investment that are not present in traditional land; monetization also requires less investment and is potentially less restrictive.

As with traditional land, the value of virtual land is based on where it is located, how much digital traffic it attracts, and how owners choose to develop the land.

Let's take a look at the fastest growing NFT play in the current market, Decentraland, as an example of the revenue-generating opportunities available to digital land investors.

According to Republic, popular developments within Decentraland include:

- Art galleries where owners can sell their NFT digital art, Cryptokitties and other NFT collectibles
- Casinos, where players can win MANA, the cryptocurrency that facilitates the purchase of digital land.
- Gaming sites

- Brand-sponsored content, such as the Atari arcade that features games that can be played in Decentraland
- Music venues where musicians can play and hold concerts

Digital land can also be leased, allowing owners to generate cash flow and income from tenants or other utilities.

For example, Alien Worlds, one of the largest digital land NFT games in the world that is run in partnership with Binance, allows players to generate real income by allowing other players to come and mine from your plot.

These are just a few examples of the monetization possibilities of digital land. As more games and platforms emerge with digital land NFTs, the sky is the limit for the type of virtual revenue landowners could pursue.

Virtual land allows the buyer to easily develop and pursue multiple revenue generation opportunities that they truly enjoy. In the virtual world, property can be built in an instant, removing all the barriers associated with distance, time and space in traditional investments.

Easy international and borderless access

As in real life, virtual real estate is about location, location, location. In both traditional and digital real estate, value is heavily influenced by location and the amount of traffic the area attracts.

With physical assets, a multitude of factors influence location and traffic that are completely out of the buyer's control.

How far or close an airport is, whether or not it has significant landmarks that attract international users and visitors, ease of access, infrastructure, regulations for international travel, and unforeseen global events such as the Covid pandemic can all play a role.

In virtual platforms, people can visit instantly from around the world with their avatars. Virtual conventions, where participants can gather to watch a sporting event, network or pitch ideas to investors in Crypto Valley, can draw a crowd and drive traffic to your location, increasing its value at no additional cost.

Annual Percentage Return and ROI

Revenue growth for video games is expected to increase from over $159.3 billion in 2020 to $189.3 billion in 2021. And from 2020 to 2027, the global industry is set for a compound annual growth rate (CAGR) of 12.9%.

And as more people and brands enter the metaverse to enjoy a unique, borderless experience and advertise to users, the value of digital land assets will continue to grow.

Compare that to the years spent obtaining planning permission and developing traditional land investments, and it's clear where the potential for higher annual percentage returns (APY) and ROI lies.

In 2018, Decentraland made headlines when digital land investors' returns soared 500%. The decentralized virtual world has continued to gain ground since then: digital land sold in early 2019 at Decentraland for $500 is now trading at over $7,860, with an ROI of 1,572%.

Decentraland's cryptocurrency, MANA, jumped in 2021 and has been in a bullish cycle for over a year. Decentraland is one of the world's most popular multiplayer games and the fastest growing blockchain, NFT and digital terrestrial virtual world.

As more players grow in the gaming ecosystem, the value of the digital asset increases. Low supply and exponentially growing demand can drive up prices.

Youtuber LiteLiger shared a few examples of NFT investments in digital land that have increased significantly in value over the course of a few months:

The Sandbox is an Ethereum-based game backed by institutional investors.

LiteLiger purchased a plot of Sandbox land for $100.

Eight months later, LiteLiger received offers to purchase $650 worth of its Sandbox land.

These phenomenal increases in digital land prices show the potential increase in valuation for digital land NFTs where the buyer purchases the land in the early stages of game development and release before it gains more significant traction in the marketplace.

Where you have a fixed amount of land on one of these platforms and it eventually attracts thousands if not millions of users, there is the potential for huge returns; the value of your digital land assets can only increase as network effects, users, and brand dominance increase.

Tips for investing in digital territory
The value of the games industry exceeds both music and movies combined. And with the largest application of NFTs in the gaming world, terrestrial digital NFTs offer a significant investment opportunity.

Early adopters will benefit from all the inbound trading taking place in the metaverse. But as with any investment, there's no guarantee that your digital asset will perform well and generate a sizable ROI.

So what are the key properties of high-growth digital land NFTs? And what are the indicators that the virtual platform is destined to grow? While there is a lot of money to be made in the NFT space, investors should understand the value drivers for an asset class before making an allocation.

How to capture NFTs that will be hot in the future and preserve long-term value

1. Will it capture network effects?

In the future, how many people will be interested in NFT? What is the most expensive NFT that the game has sold so far? How many active monthly users are there?

Will successful digital metaverses capture network effects. Will there be a high level of community involvement in the distribution mode?

2. Levels of involvement

How does the game capture user engagement and would you like to play the game for hours consistently? The more loyal and engaged the circle is, the more likely it is to attract more smart money and users outside the circle.

3.　　Utility: what will this NFT actually be able to do?

The more compelling the content is that users can interact with, the more valuable the metaverse becomes. This attracts more users, which increases the value of the NFT and attracts more interest from advertisers and sponsorships.

4.　　Guaranteed scarcity of digital land assets

Attractive digital terrain implies design rarity and guaranteed scarcity. Does the open value economy in the game work well? Do NFTs create unique and differentiated value for users? How easy is it to exchange and cash in game tokens for real currency?

As more players grow in a gaming ecosystem, the value of the digital asset increases: low supply and exponentially growing demand can drive up prices.

5.　　Team: experience, skill and track record

How skilled is the team that is building this game? Who are the game creators and how successful have they been previously?

6.   Brand value

How well known and valued is the brand? Are its digital assets interchangeable with third-party games and platforms?

7.   Market traction and player growth

Has it? been mentioned in any larger publications? Is it gaining traction? Online multiplayer games that leverage the network effect can drive player growth and become a key competitive advantage.

A user's decision to use a platform is often based on the number of other users and applications on the platform - incentives such as the in-game economy can also help tip the scales.

Prolific digital land investor Decentraland Phergyson advises to "do a little research before you buy. Even if it's the cheapest parcel on the map, it still might not be a good deal. The problem is that a lot of people come in here expecting 10X or 100X their investment, so it doesn't seem to matter to them if they pay a little more. That's one of the reasons there's so much money to be made at Decentraland.

"Once you have an idea of what the parcels of land are worth, it's pretty easy to buy at a low price and sell at market prices, or a little lower, and still make a big profit. I average about 20 percent on almost 200 sales."

If you're interested in learning about upcoming digital land sales, NFT Plazas and Play to Earn are two good news sources to keep track of the latest developments in the NFT digital land market.

Conclusion

NFT tokens are the fashion of the moment, although they have been around for several years now, albeit previously in much less evolved forms. While there is certainly fashion to push prices up, on the other hand we find a concrete application - also commercially - increasingly large for this type of product.

The emergence of many blockchains capable of supporting them - which we have adequately illustrated in the course of our guide today - tells us of an embryonic situation, but one that is rapidly gaining traction within the blockchain world and also in markets for exchanging property rights.

We're still in an extremely experimental phase of the NFT world, and the prices of some of the assets that went up for auction reflect just this extremely immature state of the technology and the markets that revolve around it. There are, however, other considerations to be made in this regard, avoiding trivialities that do not help us at all to understand the present and the future of this type of ecosystems.

They will be a very valid channel for the ownership of artistic works

We have very few doubts about this. The auctions that have already been held at Christie's and Sotheby's will pave the way for a massive entry of NFT technology into the art markets. We believe there is no doubt about it: NFTs are an intelligent, fast, secure and cost-effective way to exchange ownership of artworks, digital and otherwise.

They will be a Revolution for the world of video games

Where there were already several companies that found themselves managing complex economies, not having the possibility to delegate the exchanges to efficient third party systems like the blockchain hosting NFTs. We already have clear demonstrations that NFTs will become the standard for any kind of virtual world, present and future. And those who don't comply will end up losing a huge amount of profits.

They will also be a turning point for collectors

And there's very little to doubt about that either. We're not just talking about collections of digital works, but also of physical objects. Let's imagine, for example, the sector of collectible cards, which today sees a lot of speculators taking part in auctions. A Pokémon or Magic the Gathering card can also exceed $100,000 in value. Moving them physically is expensive and risky. When third parties emerge to guarantee the transaction, they can be kept in banks or custody services and to pass (and guarantee the passage), it will be only the NTF token that represents the ownership of the card.

For finance: OTC contracts

We enter specialist territory. The OTC market could find in the blockchain supporting NFTs an excellent support for the transfer of customized contracts, without the need to refer anymore to internal clearing houses: expensive and insecure and above all also exposed to human error. Many of the derivative investments with specific contracts could find in NFTs an excellent ally.

To understand us, there are many sectors that NFTs could revolutionize. It is not certain that they will succeed with all the sectors that at the moment are interested in this technology. But the prospects are more than interesting and open to very positive scenarios, especially for those who are now entering the market.

NFT tokens are part fad, part very interesting technological solution that will really make a difference in the management of digital and non-digital properties. Also for those who want to invest in this sector there are now two roads: to bet on exclusive works of art - and therefore speculate on their possible revaluation, or to bet on the tokens of the projects that host them. Two very different ways, that cross themselves just with NFTs.

Jeff H. Bolton
NFT Investing

www.ingramcontent.com/pod-product-compliance
Lightning Source LLC
Chambersburg PA
CBHW052357060726
47592CB00019B/1296